The Race
for the Vase

Mary Elizabeth Salzmann

Consulting Editor, Diane Craig, M.A./Reading Specialist

ABDO
Publishing Company

Published by ABDO Publishing Company, 4940 Viking Drive, Edina, Minnesota 55435.

Printed in the United States.

Credits
Edited by: Pam Price
Curriculum Coordinator: Nancy Tuminelly
Cover and Interior Design and Production: Mighty Media
Photo and Illustration Credits: BananaStock Ltd., Brand X Pictures, Comstock, Corbis Images, Eyewire Images, Hemera, Image Source, Tracy Kompelien, PhotoDisc

Library of Congress Cataloging-in-Publication Data

Salzmann, Mary Elizabeth, 1968-
        The race for the vase / Mary Elizabeth Salzmann.
          p. cm. -- (Rhyme time)
        ISBN 1-59197-813-0 (hardcover)
        ISBN 1-59197-919-6 (paperback)
        1. English language--Rhyme--Juvenile literature. I. Title. II. Rhyme time (ABDO Publishing Company)

    PE1517.S357 2004
    428.1'3--dc22

                                                                            2004050427

SandCastle™ books are created by a professional team of educators, reading specialists, and content developers around five essential components that include phonemic awareness, phonics, vocabulary, text comprehension, and fluency. All books are written, reviewed, and leveled for guided reading, early intervention reading, and Accelerated Reader® programs and designed for use in shared, guided, and independent reading and writing activities to support a balanced approach to literacy instruction.

Let Us Know

After reading the book, SandCastle would like you to tell us your stories about reading. What is your favorite page? Was there something hard that you needed help with? Share the ups and downs of learning to read. We want to hear from you! To get posted on the ABDO Publishing Company Web site, send us e-mail at:

sandcastle@abdopub.com

SandCastle Level: Fluent

Words that rhyme do
not have to be spelled the
same. These words rhyme
with each other:

bass

grace

case   lace

chase   place

erase   race

face   vase

Angelina's mom puts sunscreen on her face.

Gabriel is learning how to play bass guitar.

In ballet class, Katy and Erica learn to move with grace.

Charles will probably not fall off his bike, but he wears a helmet just in **case**.

In his sister's wedding, Donald carries the rings on a pillow trimmed with **lace**.

Thomas will throw the Frisbee for his dog to **chase**.

Tori's favorite **place** to read is in her room.

Daniel tries not to make a mistake so he won't have to erase.

Lizzie, Debra, and Morgan race across the sand.

Brittany and Richard are giving their mom breakfast in bed and a rose in a **vase**.

The Race
for the Vase

Today is the day of
Harry and Myrtle's big race.
They both want to win first place.
The prize is a splendid vase.

Not wanting to tire and lose face,
Myrtle sets a slow, steady pace.

Harry dashes far ahead in the race.
He stops to see his friend Grace.

Grace is getting married
in a veil made of lace.

Harry is still (far) ahead
in the chase,
so he takes time to listen
to Bob play his bass.

Myrtle keeps her eyes on the vase
and continues at her steady pace.

Myrtle took the lead, to Harry's disgrace.
His stalling and stopping
had cost him the race!

FINISH

Slow and steady won Myrtle first place!
She takes home the splendid vase.

Rhyming Riddle

What do you call a container for the largest violin?

Bass case

Glossary

bass. a stringed musical instrument that makes very low tones

Frisbee. a brand of plastic disk that people throw back and forth

grace. an elegant or fluid movement

splendid. very grand and beautiful

stall. to delay or put off

About SandCastle™

A professional team of educators, reading specialists, and content developers created the SandCastle™ series to support young readers as they develop reading skills and strategies and increase their general knowledge. The SandCastle™ series has four levels that correspond to early literacy development in young children. The levels are provided to help teachers and parents select the appropriate books for young readers.

Emerging Readers
(no flags)

Beginning Readers
(1 flag)

Transitional Readers
(2 flags)

Fluent Readers
(3 flags)

These levels are meant only as a guide. All levels are subject to change.

To see a complete list of SandCastle™ books and other nonfiction titles from ABDO Publishing Company, visit **www.abdopub.com** or contact us at: 4940 Viking Drive, Edina, Minnesota 55435 • 1-800-800-1312 • fax: 1-952-831-1632